The Friend Cleanse

By Dr. Leslie Dobson

Book Cover Design: Richter Publishing with stock art from RF123.com

Editors: Austin Hatch, Selena Mouzon & Abigail Bunner

Additional Contributors: Tara Richter

Publisher: Richter Publishing LLC
www.richterpublishing.com

ISBN-13: 978-1-954094-46-8

DISCLAIMER

This book is designed to provide information on healthy relationships only. This information is provided and sold with the knowledge that the publisher and author do not offer any legal, medical, or psychological advice. In the case of a need for any such expertise, consult with the appropriate professional. This book does not contain all information available on the subject. This book has not been created to be specific to any individual's or organization's situation or needs. Every effort has been made to make this book as accurate as possible. However, there may be typographical and/ or content errors. Therefore, this book should serve only as a general guide and not as the ultimate source of subject information. This book contains information that might be dated and is intended only to educate and entertain. The author and publisher shall have no liability or responsibility to any person or entity regarding any loss or damage incurred, or alleged to have incurred, directly or indirectly, by the information contained in this book. You hereby agree to be bound by this disclaimer or you may return this book within the guaranteed time period for a full refund. In the interest of full disclosure, this book may contain affiliate links that might pay the author or publisher a commission upon any purchase from the company. While the author and publisher take no responsibility for the business practices of these companies and or the performance of any product or service, the author or publisher has used the product or service and makes a recommendation in good faith based on that experience. All characters appearing in this work are fictitious. Any resemblance to real persons, living or dead, is purely coincidental. The opinions and stories in this book are the views of the author and not that of the publisher.

FOREWARD

I am so proud of my beautiful, intelligent, and amazing wife, Leslie. She is my best friend and the best mother to our two children. Leslie, I could not be more proud of the psychologist you have become, and the impact that you have on the world. We have worked in countless dangerous settings that required every ounce of our energy, and you have taught me how to hold and maintain boundaries with others throughout these experiences, and throughout our 10-year marriage. I am extremely proud of this book, and you are the inspiration for so many others to live healthy lives, with healthy boundaries, and preserve their energy to live their best lives.

Your husband, Dr. Wesley Cook

DEDICATION

I would like to dedicate this book to my husband, Dr. Wes Cook. Thank you for navigating life with me and being the best psychologist, father, and partner imaginable. Thank you for always supporting me, helping me maintain my energy, and allowing me to sparkle.

PROLOGUE

I want to take you back with me to one of the scariest moments in my life. This was a moment where I learned that when I am under intense threat and I fear for the safety of my life, my right butt cheek starts to violently shake.

I spent years working with extremely dangerous people. If you can imagine the individuals television writers would write a crime show about - I met them and I got into the nitty gritty with them. In a lot of secure settings with dangerous people, the staff wear alarms somewhere on their body and when you trigger the alarm it alerts everyone in the building to where you are. I'll never forget the first time I had to trigger my alarm. I was in a maximum-security building with over 1000 male violent individuals, and I was tucked away upstairs on a small unit with 30 recent new individuals. To get into that place you had to commit a violent felony and you had to have a diagnosis of a severe mental disorder. So, here I am, not a particularly threatening or physically strong individual. I'm also extremely naïve at times, the typical California bubbly girl, making eye contact and saying hello to anyone as if they are a saint. So, of course I'm walking around with all the criminals in front of me and I look up and I see an older psychiatrist and friend interviewing a client. I didn't think anything of it, until the client jumped out of his chair with speed like the Roadrunner and flew over the table. He started flailing his arms and punching my friend in the face, moving faster than I think I've ever moved, landing blow by blow. My friend was unconscious in seconds. I instinctually triggered my alarm as though someone else would be able to get to him faster than me. It felt like minutes, but in a matter of seconds, I lunged forward to put my body in between this horrifying beatdown. As I leapt forward, I felt air, a weightlessness, and I felt the hands of other men grabbing me, pulling me, shoving me across the room until I was against a wall. In that split second, I thought "they're going to kill my friend." To my surprise, they dove into that fight, and they apprehended the inmate that was throwing the punches, and they held him down. There were three or four men holding down just one, and they were brutally beaten up by this inmate. They took punches, blow after blow, to save that doctor, my friend. My friend was unconscious under a chair with a table fallen on him, and I just stood there and watched him to see if he was breathing. I couldn't get close enough to him. When other people arrived on scene and started to give him medical care, I noticed that his fingers were bent backwards and broken. They took him away for medical care and I was in complete and total shock. It was around 5:00 PM and I walked back to my office, and I just started crying. That was the first time in my life where I felt like I needed to help but I was also completely helpless.

So, I ask you this question, since I'm assuming you don't wear an alarm in your everyday life ... and violations against our integrity are not always physical. If there is intrusion upon you, a need for you to help someone else, or because you are the victim, how do you empower yourself to act quickly, efficiently, and save your life?

Boundaries. Boundaries from emotional and psychological manipulation of others. From physical attempts to hurt us or touch us. Boundaries from what we are called to do but we know we are not capable of doing. Boundaries that show that we are aware of our capacity, our energy, and that we are giving ourselves permission to live the life we are capable of, to make decisions to increase our energy, and to live our life and show up for ourselves.

I have been in countless situations where I have been manipulated, threatened, attacked, abused, and quite literally near death. The thread that rides through all of these experiences was my need to set boundaries within myself, and boundaries with other people, so that I was fully aware, capable, and giving myself permission to maintain my confidence, empower myself, stay calm and grounded, and live the most healthy, transparent, genuine, authentic presentation of myself.

Now, I know extreme examples shouldn't be generalized, but how do you actually do this? I want to introduce a concept to you called The Friend Cleanse. I want to give you permission to take a break from the world. Break from interpersonal interactions, social plans, pressures to be in this world. I want you to sit back and reflect on all the people you are around that are close to you in your inner circle and even distant to you at the grocery store. I want you to look at the energy that they pull from you or the energy that they give you. And I want you to look at how you show up to all those interactions, the feelings of pressure to talk to the person at the store, or feeling like you are gaining energy and feeling grounded by that one friend in your inner circle who you look forward to being with. I want you to cleanse this concept of giving everything we have to people and not setting boundaries - to preserving our energy source.

And then what I want you to do is strategically place individuals in your life around you. Now, I have this tool that I call the friend sphere on my website where you can visualize doing this exercise. First, you can visualize yourself in the middle, and then you can start moving people around you. If somebody is a drain to your energy but you have them close to you in your inner circle, you will see that your glass of energy begins to go down. But if you start to move them to the outer layers of your sphere, you will see that your glass of energy increases.

It's time to show up for yourself. To give yourself permission to be in charge of the interactions around you. You are happening to your life. Life is not happening to you.

Table of Contents

ACKNOWLEDGMENTS

I would like to thank my incredible "texting friend" of 10 years, Becky. Even though we are so far apart, our friendship means the world to me. You helped me stay authentic and true to my message.

I would like to thank my incredible "wiser friend," Maggie. You have become my family, and I am thrilled to raise our daughters together.

INTRODUCTION

The Friend Cleanse is a process to take back control of your life. Do you constantly feel drained? Not enough energy to get through the day? Are your relationships taking more from you than giving to you? Then you need a Friend Cleanse! Within this book you will discover how to identify people and their energy, and then strategically place them around your sphere based on if they add or subtract from your quality of life (i.e., energy). Your time is precious, and learning how to establish healthy boundaries is crucial to living a balanced life. It is time to save your life.

The Friend Cleanse is an opportunity to pause life and say, "I do not have to be in relationships because of pressure or force. I can stand back and say, 'This is how I want my life, and this is what I want it to look like.'" You can take control of your life by deciding who is in your inner circle, and both strategically and in your imagination, place people around you.

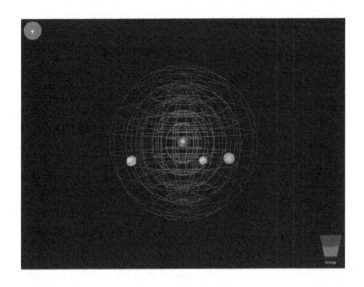

Imagination is powerful. As you step back and envision where you want the people in your life to be placed, you will begin to build awareness and take your control back. So, when you decide to let people back in, it will be an active decision, in control, in awareness, genuine, and allow you to accurately vet people before they enter or re-enter your life.

How do you vet people? First, I want you to start by identifying and defining their character and try to put a name to them so that you feel more able to quickly identify them. Naming them will allow you to decide how they impact you and your energy. You will determine when you want to see them, how frequently, and what type of relationship you want to have with them (e.g., close or distant). You can reassess this name and distance whenever you like. You can do your friend cleanse every quarter of the year, or possibly, after there has been a significant life event. You have the power, and that is a beautiful concept to incorporate into your life.

I am a forensic psychologist and I have spent over 20 years in the assessment and treatment of mental health disorders in individual and group therapy, and criminal and civil law. I learned early on how to establish strict boundaries, and how to only let certain people into my life. My day-to-day was not like the average person, where most get up, go to work from 9-5, talk around the water cooler, do work, and then go home when it is time. No, I was working in mental institutions with serial killers and people struggling with the most severe mental health disorders I have ever seen in my life. I have yet to see a movie portray my experience well, although the recent film "Joker" comes to mind. Severe mental health is often referred to as a 'disorder of horrors,' and I completely agree. With that said, I was still somewhat naïve back in those days and sometimes let the environment and the people get the best of me. I wanted to help them. I wanted to help the inmates, the patients, the staff, the system, and most of all, protect our communities. But many of the inmates and patients were very manipulative and used my caring and empathic nature to take advantage and manipulate me.

My clinical stories have been completely de-identified, but I want to be honest with you. I want you to understand the depth of psychological manipulation, so that you may understand my views on setting interpersonal boundaries. So, take it with a grain of salt.

I once worked with a man in therapy, in a maximum-security setting. I felt that we had 'therapeutic rapport', and a strong connection. I thought he was making progress with his symptoms of depression, becoming less depressed over time. I was fully engaged in helping him heal his past traumas and present depression. I was under the impression that our therapy was making a significant impact. In one session, he requested to have his bedroom moved because he claimed he was being bullied by his cellmates, which seemed entirely justified. I was proud that this strong and very antisocial man was attempting to tell me something vulnerable. He did not feel safe. I was 25 years old. I attempted to communicate with the facility staff and asked them to move the client. I explained he was having trouble sleeping due to the constant disruptions; however, things took an unexpected turn. The staff, who were working off-shift hours, eventually agreed to the room transfer, but that very night, a massive and violent riot broke out around his old room. It became evident that my client had orchestrated the entire ordeal. He manipulated individual therapy, my own perception of the relationship, leading to a massive and violent riot. He had planned this for weeks, once he saw he was "working" the facility, I became his pawn. I played a role in facilitating his request. As we worked 'together' in therapy, he was slowly orchestrating other clients in preparation to fight each other, and directly physically assault the facility staff that he knew were working off-shift the same night.

I walk the halls with individuals who committed heinous crimes, and when I enter these prisons, I often become their amusement for the day. They try to manipulate me, drain my emotions, and all my energy for their entertainment. In these environments, the only thing I have to protect myself are my boundaries. I assess people, remain vigilant, and maintain confidence in my reasons for setting my relational boundaries. The level of manipulation a person encounters when getting to know a murderer, psychopath, or even a cannibal, is incredibly meticulous.

These are extreme examples compared to everyday life; however, I learned valuable lessons in these work experiences. As much as I cared for and wanted to help these people, I always had to have my guard up. People in life can and *will* manipulate you, even in everyday, non-criminal settings. Psychopathic people walk amongst you every day. They walk by you before they are arrested, and before I get a chance to meet them. They are your neighbors, friends, colleagues, and even family members. You never know when you are sitting next to a psychopath. I will teach you tips to help you protect your energy and sanity, no matter who you come across. You will be able to identify the different traits of people within your life, actively deciding how close they get to be.

After walking the halls in dangerous environments for years, I can identify the need for a boundary faster and more efficiently than most people I know. I can place the metaphorical and imaginary boundary effectively. When I miss it, or mess it up, I am quick to resolve it. Understand that this process is not perfect. We can start with a cleanse that is like a sprint, and then we have a marathon of good choices ahead of us. It is trial and error, and it evolved into a well-versed skill in which I am proud. I spot when others need boundaries, and one of the most meaningful parts of my therapy practice involves educating and giving clients permission to set boundaries and feel in control of their lives. My clients have found this process eye-opening. When they do a friend cleanse, they feel better. They report more energy, and they are more motivated. Certain areas of their life start to take off, a force of momentum behind them, and the energy remains present for them to grab onto and continue moving forward with their dreams, hope, vision, and happiness. They have the energy because they do not have toxic people in their lives sucking them dry.

I hope more than anything that my clients never feel unlovable, helpless, or hopeless. These are very common core beliefs that people have, and I want my clients to counteract these beliefs by feeling consistent strength, confidence, and empowerment. I devote my life to the instillation of self-esteem and resiliency because people are blind to how incredible they are, like you.

I wrote this book because I want to show my journey to anyone that can benefit. I want everyone to see that with great pain comes amazing clarity and empowerment, an ability to cleanly and confidently control your life and those who are within your sphere. You can control how people impact you. Did you hear that? You can control how people impact you.

There are genuinely toxic people in this world, and they do not have to bleed into you. They do not get to suck you dry, like an energy vampire. You have the ability to set physical and emotional boundaries around yourself, and you can decide on when you care, what you care about, and how much you care ... or if you do not care at all. Can you imagine how that feels? It feels unstoppable.

Please, do not live your life in a prison. Do not put others in a prison. I want you to learn to trust your gut and your intuition, and you know you have the capacity to be as tough as a prison wall. You can be tough, while still being free flowing with your energy and your emotions, able to connect to others that deserve your presence, respect you, and fill your glass of energy in life.

Within these chapters, I am going to teach you how to

identify the good and bad people in your lives. Who gives you energy? Who takes your energy away? Where do you place these people in your sphere so you can establish boundaries and be your most authentic self?

ENERGY

Understanding Energy Within Ourselves

In the fast-paced world that we live in, it is important to maintain our energy levels. Our energy is not just physical, but also mental and emotional. It is what drives us to complete tasks, engage with others, and ultimately, live our lives.

As human beings, we have a limited amount of energy available to us. Just like how we recharge our phones and laptops, we also need to recharge ourselves in order to function optimally.

Maintaining our energy is not just about getting enough sleep or eating well - although these are important factors. It also involves managing our mental and emotional well-being.

One way to do this is by recognizing and understanding our energy levels throughout the day. We all have times when we feel more energized and productive, and other times when we feel drained and unmotivated. By paying attention to these patterns, we can schedule our tasks accordingly, maximizing our productivity and efficiency.

I use this technique in my private practice every day. I schedule my clients based on how I am feeling. I know that after I get my kids up and off to school, that I need a minute to ground myself in my office before I see a client. So, I try not to schedule a client within an hour. The awareness of this need, and meeting the need with space, grounding, and a cup of green tea, allows me to be a better therapist. It also allowed me to be more present with not only others, but myself. I can maintain my energy better throughout the rest of the day.

Energy is Like a Glass of Water

Think of yourself like a glass of water. When your glass is full is when you are full of energy. It is when you are being your most genuine and authentic self and feeling congruent in your conversations. Your plans for the day and your thoughts match perfectly. There is a moment where everything feels blissful.

Inevitably, there comes a moment where we want to help others, and we pour some of our energy into someone else's glass. That is appropriate and natural, if we have the energy to give. However, when people ask for too much, and we still oblige, our glass of energy gets too low. We do not have enough energy to take care of ourselves in a consistent and ongoing manner, and also reserve the energy to care for our immediate needs in us or very close family, such as children. If we are low on energy and we have taxed our preserve, we get tired, angry, fuzzy in our thoughts, and we are not congruent in our actions anymore. We are not the most genuine and authentic presentation of ourselves.

Maintaining our energy is a vital aspect of overall well-being. By recognizing and managing our energy levels and prioritizing self-care, we can cultivate a healthy and sustainable level of energy to thrive in all areas of our lives. Remember to pay attention to your energy patterns and make adjustments when needed. With this in mind, you can take control of your energy and live a fulfilling and balanced life.

I once had a friend who asked a lot of me. She would often ask for help with her schoolwork, childcare, and even financial advice at times. I was new to the area, and I wanted to make friends, so I ignored the feeling of being used and drained when I was in her presence. As time went on, the feeling of being taken advantage of and drained after interactions with her got bigger and bigger. I struggled with the need to set a boundary because I felt lonely living in a new area; however, when I decided to finally set the boundary, it freed up my energy to engage in more meaningful relationships with people that increased my energy rather than draining it.

Maintaining Our Energy

Self-care is a crucial aspect of maintaining our energy. This includes taking time for ourselves to relax and recharge, whether it be through exercise, meditation, or simply doing something we enjoy. It is important to note that people need a consistent support system, and that is not necessarily other people. A consistent support system can be a healthy routine on which you can rely. For me, I use Pilates. I find it challenging, strengthening, and it allows my energy to be filled, without draining me. Of course, there is usually one or two days a month where I do not attend my Pilates class, and that is because I did not balance my energy well, or something surprised me in life that drained me, and I know that if I exert physical and social energy at the gym, I will not have enough left for my work, family, and self. That is a decision I make, and staying home with solitude and rest is usually the best way to increase my energy.

It also means being mindful of our mental and emotional needs and addressing them in a healthy way. People take away from our glass of energy. We must be mindful of the people we keep within our sphere and how much we allow them to zap our energy resources, even if it is someone you see at the gym for a brief period, but you know it taxes your resources.

By prioritizing self-care, we are able to replenish our energy reserves and prevent burnout. This allows us to continue functioning at our best and be more present in all aspects of our lives.

On the next page, I want to show you different images of a glass of water. On the empty glass, write down the items or people that take energy away from you. How do you feel after your interactions? Do you feel drained?

What Takes Energy Away?

1. _____
2. _____
3. _____
4. _____
5. _____
6. _____
7. _____
8. _____
9. _____
10. _____
11. _____
12. _____

More thoughts and reflections on what empties your energy cup:

_____

_____

_____

_____

_____

_____

_____

_____

_____

_____

_____

_____

What Adds Energy?

1._____
2._____
3._____
4._____
5._____
6._____
7._____
8._____
9. _____
10._____
11._____
12. _____

More thoughts and reflections on what add to your energy cup:

_____

_____

_____

_____

Maintaining our energy is a vital aspect of overall well-being. By recognizing and managing our energy levels, avoiding energy vampires, and prioritizing self-care, we can cultivate a healthy and sustainable level of energy to thrive in all areas of our lives. Remember to pay attention to your energy patterns and make adjustments when needed. With this in mind, you can take control of your energy and live a fulfilling and balanced life.

Keep in mind that everyone's energy levels are unique and may differ from day to day. It is important to listen to your body and mind, as they will give you cues on when to take a break or seek help. Remember, self-care is not selfish, and it is necessary for maintaining our energy and overall well-being. Make sure to prioritize it in your daily routine and watch your energy and quality of life improve. If you are starting to get pulled from your true self, then the energy is not going towards you; it is going towards someone or something else. If energy is not going toward yourself, you may have less ability to know what you want and need in order to be healthy. When you feel the most healthy, you will engage with others and build meaningful and sustainable relationships. The Energy Glass helps us envision this concept. When we feel the fullest, we feel like we can do anything as the most genuine and authentic representation of ourselves.

Energy As Percentages %

I like to think of energy as percentages. I use this technique with my clients and myself frequently. You need to assess your energy levels during the day and be able to quantify them. If you quantify them, then you will have a better idea of how much energy you have to give others. For example, if you come home from work and the kids are really needy, you can say to your spouse, "Honey, right now I only have 30%, but if I take 20 minutes to be alone and ground myself, I can bring my percentage back up and then I can be fully present with you and the kids." Asking someone where they are at with their energy levels and if you can pick up some slack to help them out, so they can recharge their batteries, is a great way to utilize energy percentages as being empathetic to someone. It works both ways. Oftentimes, helping someone increase their energy will in turn increase your satisfaction, happiness, and energy.

We can also use the percentages chart by structuring interactions with people prior to spending time with them. If we know someone is going to try to take a significant percentage of our energy, we can plan accordingly beforehand. How much time do you really want to spend with that person? How many days of the week or month do you already see them? Do you want to limit it to lunch so you can spend an hour or less, then make an excuse to leave early? How are you going to navigate the interaction? Do you only need to discuss certain topics? Setting specific limits with people beforehand will help you protect your energy.

Think of your glass of energy throughout the day. Imagine how much energy you have at different given times. Do you have more energy in the morning? If so, then maybe that is the time when you can schedule certain events that will take more energy from you. Or maybe you are a night owl, so doing nighttime activities is best. Being aware of your energy and the time you can give yourself will help you avoid burnout as well.

TYPES OF FRIENDS

In this chapter, we are going to categorize the different types of friends or relationships you have in your life. Now that you have a good understanding of your energy, getting to know the personalities of the people closest to you is crucial in helping keep your glass of energy full. In today's fast-paced world, the importance of having a supportive circle of friends cannot be overstated. However, not all friendships are built on trust and mutual understanding. In some cases, we may find ourselves in toxic friendships that can have a negative impact on our mental health and well-being. Some friends exhibit unhealthy behaviors that can be harmful and draining to others. These individuals tend to bring negativity, drama, and chaos into our lives, making it difficult for us to maintain a healthy relationship with them. Toxic friends can be difficult to recognize, especially when we have known them for a long time. However, there are certain warning signs that can help us identify toxic behavior in our friends.

There are also healthy friends too, the ones that are always there for us, by lending a compassionate ear. Whenever I have good news or something I am excited about, I have one friend that I cannot wait to share it with because she will text a reply such as, "That is amazing. I love having more reasons to celebrate you!" And I feel the same way about her. We need to weed out the good from bad, the healthy from the unhealthy, and then learn where to place them in our personal sphere as to only allow them to take up so much space in our life. First, let's define common types of friends:

Texting Friend: This person will always text you but will not meet in person. Setting the expectation that they are just a texting friend can prevent disappointment and energy drain. By defining this relationship, receiving a text can be enjoyable without draining energy when you don't get a deeper interaction. It is hard to say if this relationship is negative or positive, as texting is very meaningful to some people, and other people simply do not enjoy texting. The key is to set the expectation for the friendship ahead of time, maintain awareness and reality in the relationship, and then nothing will catch you by surprise and drain your energy while you recover from the unpleasant emotions.

Deep Conversation Once a Year Friend: Sometimes you have a profound moment with someone, but then they disappear, and this can feel disappointing and confusing. Defining this friend as an occasional deep interaction can help manage expectations and maintain energy. It might help you to limit the personal things you share with this friend or know that once a year you can have a great and meaningful conversation with them. They may not have the capacity for a more frequent relationship, and once a year may be extremely meaningful to them. They may prioritize their family or other people, and simply see you in life when they have the energy.

Lighthearted, Won't Go Deep Friend: These friends are always up for lighthearted engagements, but won't offer deep emotional support. Defining this helps you understand the nature of the relationship and set appropriate expectations. They might be emotionally immature and cannot offer the deep conversations you need. Knowing that and keeping them for fun interactions will keep you from disappointment. This friend would be great to attend events or parties with, as the setting will allow you to enjoy each other, but it will not require deep conversation. If you avoid feeling this rift in the friendship because you have a realistic expectation, then you can preserve your energy.

Gossip Friend: The ones who engage in harmful gossip. This isn't a healthy relationship and keeping them around is not advisable. They should be moved to the outer sphere to avoid harm. If they are talking about people to you, they are most likely talking about you as well. Life is short, and I suggest spending your important energy on a more meaningful relationship. Even if it feels good to gossip with them about others, it will only leave you burnt in the end.

Not-Really-A-Friend: This is someone you'd like to be friends with, but who doesn't have your best interests in mind. They may belittle you, make demoralizing comments, or be jealous of your success. Recognizing the red flags is crucial to protect your well-being. And do not worry, if you set a boundary with a not-really-a-friend, you will have more time and energy to bring a good friend into your life.

Energy Vampire Friend: This could be a friend or a family member, even a co-worker. They tend to zap the energy out of every situation. They are only looking out for themselves and are very selfish.

An example would be the friend that calls you up to vent about their crappy day and unloads on you. As soon as they are finished and you have sympathized with their situation, it's your turn to share some news, and suddenly they have to run and hang up the phone. This person is always taking and never giving in return. You always feel drained after an interaction. The best thing to do is avoid them at all costs. Don't answer the phone when they call! If this is a family member, you have the ability to not engage with them, or you can set boundaries ahead of time, such as preventing time alone with them, always having a task to focus on, not listening to them vent, wearing headphones, having your partner or friend prevent an interaction, or being assertive with your communication of your boundary.

Bad at Reaching Out, but Responsive Friend: This is a friend that is consistent and stable but cannot initiate contact with you. They want to hear from you and think about you, but they just can't seem to initiate contact. You should only have one or two of these kinds of people around because it is draining to be the initiator in all relationships. Your energy will grow when your overall relationships are of give and take, when people in your life initiate interactions with you as much as you do them.

Socially Anxious Friend: They want to be with you but have so much anxiety about social situations and communication. It can range from just talking or maintaining eye contact to leaving their house or attending social engagements. So, you need to consider how often you're willing to make the effort to meet them and if it's worth it. It will take a lot of energy to meet up with them because you will be more worried about making them feel comfortable rather than yourself. It's ok to be friends with someone like this, just limit the amount of time you can give them. Analyze how much energy you have left after hanging out with them. Is this something you can handle once a month, once every 6 months?

No Social Skills Friend: They love you and would do anything for you, but they lack social skills, and it feels like your job is to teach them how to be an equal player in life. You can do that, if it's working and you enjoy the relationship, but it can also be draining. Depending on your environment, these dynamics can vary, so it's important to consider your specific context. Maybe you limit the interactions to certain situations. For example, you wouldn't bring that friend to your law firm's work party. You can hang with them on a weekend by yourselves, just not with other groups of people because they wouldn't understand. The thing is, you can have multiple groups of friends, but it doesn't mean that they will all get along.

Wiser Friend: Somebody who you can trust. They really, genuinely love you and care about you. They actively listen to you and your responses. This may be somebody who only fills your cup. They don't drain you at all. You know that you can place them close to you, and you can reach out to them as a way to fill your energy when you need it. They're at peace with themselves and they don't need anything from you. Having people like that around you is very healthy. They want to help you without anything in return.

Mentor Friend: Someone who has more experience in life than you, who isn't jealous of your accomplishments. They will usually give you solid advice when you ask for it and don't want anything in return other than wanting you to succeed. We all need at least one mentor in our lives.

Uncomfortable Friend: This is a person you know, and something is just off. Your other friends might even say they are weird. They give you a funny vibe and you never quite know where you stand with them. One day they are your best friend, then the next day they vanish off the face of the earth. When you do hang out with them, they might stand too close, or touch you inappropriately. You honestly don't know if they are being friendly or hitting on you or just plain creepy. You should always trust your instincts. If someone makes you uncomfortable, they are not a friend. You are experiencing red flags, and you should listen to your intuition.

Negative Nancy Friend: They never have anything good to say. They can turn your happy mood into devastation in a heartbeat. They don't solve problems, they create them. They are super draining to be around because they are never happy, and they want everyone to be miserable with them. Don't allow them to sap your joy.

Long Distance Friend: Distance doesn't matter in this friendship. You may go 10 years without talking to or seeing this person, but once you do, it's like no time has passed. This could be a friend from school or college when you were younger. Now you have moved away, gotten married, had kids, and you both know life gets in the way. But you don't hold that against each other. If you called them crying about something that happened, they would talk to you and comfort you all night. These friendships last a lifetime and are precious. My long-distance friend is in New Jersey, and even after not seeing each other for 10 years, I had a family emergency, and she was on the next flight to see me. I would do the same for her in a second. We went 10 years without seeing each other, but we texted and spoke often over the years. When I saw her, it was like no time had passed.

Control Freak Friend: They mean well, and always have the best intentions, yet don't know how to let go. Usually, they are type A personalities who come in and get shit done. Sometimes we need that in our lives, especially if we are depressed, and need a strong friend to swoop in and take over. However, sometimes they don't know when to back down or lighten up. Having good boundaries with this friend is crucial, when to allow them to help and when to tell them they have done enough.

Party Friend: This friend loves to party! There is a special place for them in your life. If you want to go out, have fun and blow off some steam, you know who to call; however, this friend cannot have deep conversations or meaningful interactions with you, showing up only during the social events in your life. They are down for the party. This friend might be self-medicating with alcohol or socializing for other things that are going on in life, so you cannot expect them to be there authentically for yours. It is important to set a boundary in your mind, and realize what type of friendship you can have now and over time.

Invalidating Friend: Somebody who is very internally focused and sometimes unempathetic. When you talk, you may feel put down, belittled, invalidated, or that they're just overly harsh and unconcerned with your feelings. If you are aware of your lack of energy, I would stay away from that friend because it takes energy to not feel looted by someone who is very selfish or internally focused. But when you have a lot of energy and you are feeling good and confident, then that is a friend you could seek out and connect with. But if you have high stress, and if you are tired or hungover or it is a Monday, then distance yourself. You will need to actively decide when you interact with them, because they may not be dismissive or invalidating from a negative place. It's because they're just very, very internally focused, probably high leaders who lack empathy and compassion in certain conversations.

There are probably more types of friends you have in your life; this list isn't all the types of people out there. And remember, people will exist differently in other's lives. Sometimes the compassionate person in your cousins' life is a narcissistic one in yours. People shift, change, and move as well depending upon what they are going through. If someone just experienced a trauma in their life, they will not be able to show up authentically for a while. Being compassionate for others as well as yourself will help maintain your energy. Remember, healthy relationships are built on mutual respect, trust, and support. Do not be afraid to speak up and set boundaries for yourself to maintain a positive and healthy friendship.

If you have other types of friendships impacting your life, write them down here:

_____

_____

_____

_____

_____

_____

_____

_____

_____

_____

FRIEND SPHERE

We have identified the types of people in your life. It is important to know who the players are first so you can strategically place them around you, and decide how much space, time, and energy to give them. If you can imagine yourself in the center of a sphere, you can place people around you in different areas of that sphere based on how much they add to your glass of energy or drain energy away from it. For example, the people that add to it and give you energy would be within your inner sphere. The energy vampires and negative people would be on the outer sphere. There are some people that maybe after the evaluation, don't deserve a spot in your world at all.

You can do this exercise as often as you need to. Sometimes a new person will come into your life, and it will take a bit to identify where they fit within your sphere. You might really like them at first and immediately put them into your inner circle. Then after a few months, it just doesn't feel right. They are taking more than giving and you need to move them to the outer areas to protect your energy. It is important to enter every relationship slowly and understand the person, but if things go south, you can always change the relationship and reestablish a fitting boundary.

On the next page, there is an example of what the exercise will look like. There is an interactive sphere on my website where you can do this.

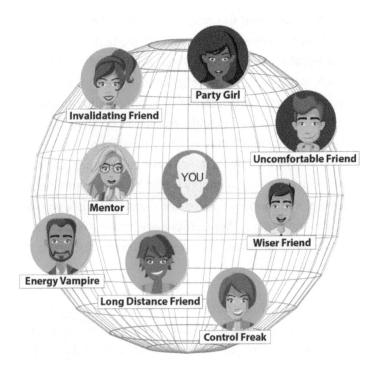

Now let's write out and categorize the people in your life. What category do you believe they fit into? You may have multiple people in one slot and none for another and that's okay. Writing it out may help you see where you are lacking in support. Maybe you are full of energy vampires and have no mentors. Visualizing this will help you make positive changes to help you in the future.

Texting Friend:

_____

_____

_____

Deep Conversation Once a Year Friend:

_____

_____

_____

Lighthearted, Won't Go Deep Friend:

_____

_____

Gossip Friend:

_____

_____

_____

Not-Really-A-Friend:

_____

_____

_____

Energy Vampire Friend:

_____

_____

_____

Bad at Reaching Out, but Responsive Friend:

_____

_____

_____

Socially Anxious Friend:

_____

_____

_____

No Social Skills Friend:

_____

_____

_____

Wiser Friend:

_____

_____

_____

Mentor Friend:

_____

_____

_____

Uncomfortable Friend:

_____

_____

_____

Negative Nancy Friend:

_____

_____

_____

Long Distance Friend:

_____

_____

_____

Control Freak Friend:

_____

_____

_____

Party Friend:

_____

_____

_____

Invalidating Friend:

_____

_____

_____

You can use the interactive friend sphere tool on my website to organize the people in your life according to how much time you want to interact with them. Go here: www.drlesliedobson.com

ATTACHMENT STYLES

Attachment styles refer to the way that individuals form and maintain emotional bonds with others. These styles are developed early in life through interactions with caregivers and can greatly influence how individuals approach relationships throughout their lives. Psychologist John Bowlby first introduced attachment theory in the 1960s, and since then, it has been widely studied and applied in various fields, such as parenting, relationships, and therapy.

There are many descriptions and types of attachment styles in psychology research, but I prefer the four main attachment styles: secure, avoidant-dismissive, ambivalent, and disorganized. Each style is characterized by different patterns of behavior and emotion when it comes to forming and maintaining relationships. Understanding these types of attachments and which one feels similar to how you are attaching to others, will help you improve your overall relationships in your life, and understand what boundaries you need to set with certain people. It should be noted that our attachment styles change over time, and they change with different people depending on their attachment style. It's an understanding that you can reflect on over and over in life, taking time to reassess the topic frequently.

Disorganized Attachment

People with this style often have inconsistent or confusing patterns of behavior in relationships. This may be due to experiencing trauma or neglect during early childhood, leading to difficulty with regulating emotions and forming secure attachments. People with this attachment style may experience fear, confusion, and anger towards others, making it difficult for them to trust and form secure relationships in life.

Avoidant-Dismissive Attachment

People with an avoidant-dismissive attachment style often have a dismissive attitude towards relationships. They may appear emotionally distant or disconnected from others, and they tend to avoid intimacy and emotional vulnerability. This may be due to having caregivers who were unresponsive or unavailable during childhood, leading to a fear of rejection and a belief that their needs will not be met in relationships. This may be due to their tendency to dismiss their own emotions and needs, as well as the emotions and needs of others. They may appear emotionally detached and self-sufficient, but in reality, they often fear rejection and abandonment.

Secure Attachment

This attachment style allows for positive and healthy patterns of behavior in relationships. People with secure attachments are able to form strong emotional bonds with others, trust easily, and communicate effectively. This is likely because they had people in their lives growing up that were consistently responsive and nurturing, providing a secure base for them to explore the world and form healthy relationships.

Ambivalent Attachment

People with an ambivalent attachment style often have a preoccupation with relationships and may struggle with feelings of anxiety, insecurity, and jealousy. This may be due to having inconsistent or unpredictable relationships during childhood, leading to a fear of abandonment and difficulty regulating emotions in adult relationships. They may also have a tendency to become overly dependent on their partners, seeking constant reassurance and validation.

While attachment styles are generally formed in early childhood and can be difficult to change, it is not impossible. With self-awareness and a willingness to work on yourself, we can develop more secure attachments and improve our relationships and implementation of healthy relational boundaries. Therapy, mindfulness practices, and building healthy relationships with supportive people can all play a role in breaking the cycle of unhealthy attachment styles making their way into adult relationships.

Remember, it is never too late to break the cycle and build a stronger, more secure attachment for yourself. Take the first step towards building healthier relationships and improving your emotional intelligence. You can break the cycle of insecure attachments and strive towards a more secure and fulfilling life. Let's make the effort to work on ourselves and our relationships, for a better future. Remember, we have the power to change and grow, even in areas as complex as attachment styles. The journey may not be easy, but it will be worth it in the end. Be open to recognizing patterns in your past relationships, how your childhood experiences may have influenced them, and actively work towards developing healthier attachment styles. Only then can we truly experience the love and support that we all deserve.

SETTING BOUNDARIES

We have identified the types of personalities of different people and where to put them in your sphere of life. However, sometimes you can't just cut out people in real life like you can on a chart. What if this person is a family member, or co-worker, or another parent at your kids' school? How do you place these people at a psychological distance and protect your energy? → By establishing healthy boundaries.

Before we dive into why setting boundaries is important, let's define what boundaries actually are. Boundaries are limits that we set for ourselves and others in order to maintain a sense of personal safety, emotional well-being, and respect. They can be physical, emotional, or even psychological.

For example, you may have physical boundaries when it comes to your personal space – not allowing anyone to invade your personal space without your consent. Emotional boundaries could involve not tolerating disrespectful or manipulative behavior from others. Psychological boundaries may relate to not engaging in negative self-talk or setting unrealistic expectations for yourself.

Types of Boundaries

Physical Boundaries: These refer to boundaries related to physical touch or space. This could involve not allowing others to touch you without your consent, or not allowing them to invade your personal space.

Emotional Boundaries: These boundaries refer to protecting our emotional well-being. This could involve not tolerating disrespectful or manipulative behavior from others, or not engaging in relationships that are emotionally draining. Communicate your emotional needs with others and set boundaries around how others can treat you.

Psychological Boundaries: These relate to our thoughts and beliefs about ourselves. This could involve not engaging in negative self-talk or setting unrealistic expectations for ourselves.

Material Boundaries: These boundaries involve our material possessions. This could include setting limits on who can borrow our belongings or how much we are willing to spend on others. For example, is there a friend that every time you go out, they somehow "forget" their wallet and you have to pay? They are taking advantage of your kind nature to pick up the tab. If it happens once, no biggie, but if it's a reoccurring event or you notice the pattern, you may need to move this friend to an outer sphere.

Time Boundaries: These relate to managing our time effectively and efficiently. This could involve saying no to commitments that do not align with our priorities or setting aside time for self-care and personal growth. Limiting the amount of time you spend with certain people. It is important to communicate clearly when you are available for work-related activities and when you need personal time. This could include setting specific work hours, not taking on extra tasks outside of those hours, and not sacrificing your personal time for work. We hear "work-life balance" all the time, but what does that mean? How can you set up your overall life to maintain energy in a balanced way?

Tips for Setting Boundaries

Know Your Limits: It is important to identify your own needs and limitations before setting boundaries. This will help you communicate them clearly and effectively. As I write this, my kids are dancing and screaming behind me. Although they are very happy, it is draining my energy to hear so much noise and to have large amounts of stimulation around me. When we go out later, I know that I cannot go to noisy places. My noise energy is too low. That is a limit. Limits can be anything.

Communicate Openly: Be direct and honest when communicating your boundaries. Avoid being passive-aggressive or expecting others to read your mind. If you are not communicating in a way that feels open, why not? Can you learn more about yourself or the other person and how they may be impacting you? Are you different around other people?

Be Assertive: Setting boundaries requires being assertive and standing up for yourself. This may feel uncomfortable at first, but it's important to be firm in your boundaries. Assertive communication will allow you to express your boundaries in an honest and respectful manner. Have you ever been asked out on a date, but you are not interested? You can communicate an assertive boundary by stating, "I hear that you are interested in me romantically, but I am not available." Remain confident and listen to their reply … only if you want. You gave your answer, and you do not need to give them any more energy.

Saying "No": "No" is a crucial word in our vocabulary. I think many people forget that it is a complete sentence.

It is okay to turn down tasks or projects that do not align with your workload or values. It is okay to turn down social events, and to call out peer pressure. It is also important to say no to requests for your time or resources when you are feeling overwhelmed or drained. If you are a people pleaser, get used to saying "no" more often. Once you get in the habit of it, it gets easier, and actually becomes empowering, allowing you to maintain a sense of confidence longer and more consistently! Every time you say "no", to something or someone, you are saying "yes" to yourself, and maintaining or increasing your energy.

Practice Self-Care: This involves taking care of yourself. Make sure to prioritize self-care activities such as exercise, relaxation, and spending time with loved ones. Keep a routine that allows you to feel grounded and healthy, and available to connect with yourself and others in your life. There are so many amazing self-care ideas on the internet and in self-help books. Personally, I follow a lot of therapists, psychologists, psychiatrists, and life coaches on Instagram, and I find their content very inspiring. As I scroll social media, I am reminded to fit in self-care in my day because the accounts I follow are highly focused on self-care.

Be Consistent: Boundaries are only effective if they are consistently enforced. Stick to your boundaries and don't bend them for others. You can hold a firm boundary, while still being flexible with life's challenges and changes. Imagine the boundary in your head or on paper and know that if you are being pulled too far away from it, you can return to the boundary. Do a friend cleanse for yourself whenever you lack congruence with your true self.

Seek Support: If you struggle with setting boundaries, seek support from trusted friends or a therapist who can offer guidance and encouragement. Educate yourself, because you are too important to let people walk on you.

Reflect and Adjust: Setting boundaries is an ongoing process. Take time to reflect on how your boundaries are working for you and make adjustments as needed. If a person is draining our energy, our boundary will be that they need to be around us less, maybe fewer days a month or maybe when we do see them, we limit the minutes. We may limit what we are willing to converse about.

Ultimately, setting boundaries leads to a happier and more fulfilling life. By prioritizing your own well-being and taking control of your relationships, you can create a more positive and fulfilling life for yourself. So don't be afraid to set boundaries and stand up for yourself, it's an important aspect of self-care and personal growth. Start practicing setting boundaries today and see the positive impact it can have on your life! Remember, boundaries are not about being selfish or rude, but rather they are a way to protect and take care of yourself, which is essential for living a happy and healthy life. Be kind to yourself and set those boundaries!

How does this look in the real world? Here are some examples:

1) Sally's cousin only calls her to dish out the family gossip, find out what drama is going on in her life, and never really seems happy for her. Sally called her to share some amazing news that she got a huge job promotion, but to Sally's dismay, her cousin blew it off and said she probably only got the job because she slept with the boss, and then she laughed hysterically. This really hurt Sally's feelings and she confronted her cousin. Of course, the cousin was defensive and said Sally was being overly sensitive, and she was only joking, but never really congratulated her on the new job. Sally responded that if she couldn't be happy for her and be serious, she no longer wanted to talk. Her cousin started yelling incoherently, so Sally hung up the phone on her. She knew she could no longer share happy news with her negative cousin and had to put her at arm's length from now on even though she was family. Sally attempted to set a soft boundary and use assertive communication, but her cousin was not receptive. It was necessary for Sally to set a firm boundary by hanging up the phone, giving her the ability to reflect on the

relationship and assess future boundaries.

2) Bob let Sam borrow his 2nd car. Bob and Sam had been friends for over 5 years, so it was no big deal to let his friend borrow his other car. Bob's spare car was one he let his mother use when she visited. Sam's own car seemed to be taking way too long to get fixed. Four months go by and now Bob needs the car back because his mother is coming back to visit. He calls Sam to get the car back and Sam says he can't give the car back because he's driving it to North Carolina for Thanksgiving. Bob is livid because Sam never asked for permission to do this, and he needs his car back now. Sam took advantage of Bob's friendship and giving nature. Bob eventually gets the car back but knows he can never let Sam borrow any material possessions again without strict deadlines of when and how long he can use them. Bob may not even let Sam borrow the car ever again, but Bob needs space from Sam in order to reassess his boundary. Bob realized that he did not make his boundaries clear in the beginning, and he will change that in future relationships, as well.

3) The budding entrepreneur is working her butt off building a new business and it's becoming very successful. People in the area and on social media are starting to take notice of the success.

Strangers come out of the woodwork wanting to meet with the entrepreneur to buy her coffee. The naïve new business owner meets people at the coffee shop and slowly realizes these people are trying to take intellectual property from her brain, and she is drained by the interactions, knowing she is not getting anything in return. She decided to set boundaries around the meeting requests, vet the people who ask her to meet, give herself permission to value herself and identify her worth, and she set a fee structure in place for any potential opportunists. She offered them a coaching package that started at $100,000 if they wanted to learn her secrets to success. With the new boundary, she was able to preserve her energy as well as increase it because she was valued for her time, making more money, allowing her to work less.

4) A relatable example for parents is often school drop off – "Do you have the energy to stay after dropping off your children and talk with the other moms? If you do, what moms will fill your energy cup? How long should you talk? What topics? If you don't have the energy, make a plan to politely get out of there with minimal engagement (i.e., wear sunglasses, be on your phone, earbuds in). It is appropriate and healthy to honor your boundaries in all settings, and you should give yourself permission to sustain your

energy, making decisions that prevent your glass of energy from being drained.

Social Media

You have all these amazing skills with boundaries and are actively using them, however, that annoying person you don't even know keeps popping up on your social media feed. You know, the one who is always spewing their political agenda or religious stance like nails on a chalkboard. You don't agree with anything they post, and it takes your energy to ignore them. Simply seeing the posts makes you feel negative and drained, lowering your glass of energy by at least 20%. Is it worth it? Can you set a better boundary?

How to Establish Boundaries on Social Media

Identify Your Comfort Level: Take some time to reflect on what you feel comfortable sharing on social media. Consider your values, beliefs, and personal boundaries. Some people share pictures of their kids, some just their pets, and some people only use it for business purposes. Identify what you want to share with the world, and the access that the online world has to you.

Adjust Privacy Settings: Most social media platforms allow users to customize their privacy settings. Take advantage of these features to control who can see your posts and personal information.

Be Mindful of Who You Accept as Connections or Friends: It's okay to be selective about who you allow into your online social sphere. You have the right to decline friend requests or unfollow/unfriend individuals whose content may not align with your values. However, be aware that people can still follow your public page even if you do not accept them as a friend. They will only see the things you post as public. Setting your personal page to private is a healthy boundary.

Block: Use this feature freely. If someone violates your boundaries, block them. Even if they realize you have blocked them, it is important for you to remember that you chose to block their account because it was the interpersonal boundary you needed to set in order to maintain health and energy. Write your thoughts in a journal or on a post-it note, in case you need to remind yourself of your strength, reasoning, and value at a later time.

Hide Their Posts: Maybe you don't want to completely block the energy-draining person just yet, but you decide to hide their updates from your newsfeed. Hiding or muting a person's social media is a boundary and you can reassess the boundary again in the future.

Notifications: I personally like to disable all notifications for social media on my cell phone because I find them intrusive. I prefer to see things on social media when I decide to open the apps, not when the app decides to tell me. That is my boundary. Set aside time to specifically go and check your social media accounts and limit the amount of time you spend on social media. A boundary would be only checking during your lunchtime or on your train commute home after school or work.

LEARN HOW TO SAY "NO"

How to Say "No" to People: Protect Your Energy

Saying "no" can be difficult for many people. We often feel obligated to say "yes," even when we don't want to. Whether it's because we are afraid of hurting someone's feelings or we simply don't want to disappoint them, saying "no" can leave us feeling guilty and drained.

But the truth is, saying "no" is necessary for our own well-being. We need to protect our energy and prioritize ourselves in order to live a happy and healthy life. In this section, we will discuss how to say "no" in a way that is respectful and effective while still protecting our own energy.

Why Saying "No" is Important

Saying "no" allows us to set boundaries and take care of ourselves. It is not selfish or rude, it's necessary. When we constantly say "yes" to others, we often neglect our own needs and desires. This can lead to resentment, stress, and burnout. By learning how to say "no", we can protect our energy and prevent these negative feelings from building up. We'll also have more time and energy to focus on the things that truly matter to us.

How to Say "No" Effectively

Be Honest and Direct: When saying "no", it is important to be honest and direct. Don't make excuses or beat around the bush. Simply state your reason for declining and stand firm in your decision.

Offer an Alternative: If you're saying "no" to a request or invitation, offer an alternative solution. This shows that you still care and are willing to help in a different way.

Use "I" Statements: Instead of blaming the other person or making them feel guilty, use "I" statements to explain why you're saying "no". For example, "I need to prioritize my workload right now," instead of "You always ask me for help."

Practice Saying "No": Saying "no" can be difficult, especially if you're used to always saying "yes." Practice with a friend or family member, so you feel more confident and comfortable when the time comes.

Protecting Your Energy

In addition to learning how to say "no", it is important to actively protect your energy on a daily basis. This can help prevent burnout and maintain a healthy work-life balance.

Here are some ways to protect your energy:

Set Boundaries: Know your limits and communicate them to others. Do not be afraid to say no when someone asks for more than you can handle. First, analyze what you have on your plate. If taking on that additional task gives you anxiety, then maybe it is time to pass on it.

Take Breaks: Make sure to take breaks throughout the day, whether it's going for a walk, practicing deep breathing, or simply stepping away from your work for a few minutes. You can let that call go to voicemail and plan a time to listen to all your messages at once. If someone likes to drain your energy by talking on the phone for hours on end, maybe you just text them back instead of returning the call. Instead of being a sponge, try and spend time as a pumice stone.

Prioritize Self-Care: Make time for activities that bring you joy and recharge your batteries. It's not selfish to prioritize your own well-being. You might need to schedule time to do something fun like hiking, kayaking, or soaking in the hot tub. I love watching Bravo television shows.

Surround Yourself with Positive People: The people we surround ourselves with can have a big impact on our energy. Choose to spend time with those who uplift, support, and inspire you.

Listen to Your Body: Pay attention to how your body feels and honor its needs. If you're feeling tired or overwhelmed, take a break or schedule some time for self-care. Even a short 20-minute rest can help reset your brain. You can partially cleanse the chaos of the day and do a reset.

By learning to say "no" and actively protecting your energy, you can create a healthier and more balanced life for yourself. Remember that it's okay to put yourself first and prioritize your well-being. Saying "no" to others means saying "yes" to yourself and your own needs. Practice setting boundaries and taking care of yourself, and you will see your energy levels improve more consistently. You will feel more empowered in all aspects of your life. Go ahead, start saying "no" and protecting your energy. Remember, learning how to say "no" is not about being selfish or uncaring. It's about valuing your own needs and ensuring that you have the energy to take care of yourself and those around you in the best way possible. So don't be afraid to say "no" when needed, and always remember to prioritize self-care and protect your precious energy.

Let's make a commitment together to prioritize our well-being and practice saying "no" when needed. Let's create lives filled with balance, self-care, and positive energy. Remember, it's important to communicate your boundaries clearly and respectfully when saying no. Be honest about your limitations and offer alternative solutions if possible. Practice saying "no" assertively but kindly and remember that it's okay to decline requests or invitations that do not align with your needs and priorities. Protecting your energy starts with setting boundaries and learning to say "no" when needed. Don't forget to surround yourself with supportive and understanding individuals who respect your boundaries and encourage you to take care of yourself. Next time you feel overwhelmed or drained, take a moment to reflect on your priorities and boundaries, and don't be afraid to say "no" when you need to. Your well-being and energy are worth protecting. By setting clear boundaries and saying "no," we can create more space for the things that truly matter to us, leading to a more fulfilling life overall.

DECIDING WHEN TO LET GO

Friendships are an important part of our lives, providing us with companionship, support, and connection; however, not all friendships are meant to last forever. Sometimes, we may find ourselves in toxic relationships that drain our energy and do more harm than good.

But how do we know when it's time to let go of a friendship? It can be a difficult decision, especially when we have invested time and energy into the relationship. Holding onto toxic friendships can be detrimental to our well-being in the long run. If you have been practicing placing certain people in your sphere to protect your energy, yet they somehow keep creeping back in, even though you have set up firm boundaries, it might be time to end the relationship. Not everyone deserves to take up time and space in your life. You have the power to determine who gets YOU. If they disrespect you, they don't get to have you.

One way to determine if a friendship is worth letting go is by evaluating how it makes us feel. Do we leave interactions with this friend feeling drained, anxious, or upset? Do we constantly question their loyalty or intentions? If the answer is yes, then it may be a sign that the friendship is not adding positive value to our lives.

Another factor to consider is how much effort we are putting into the relationship compared to the other person. Are we always making plans, initiating conversations, or trying to keep in touch while our friend seems disinterested or distant? Friendships should be a two-way street, with both parties putting in effort and showing mutual care and interest. If we find ourselves constantly chasing after someone who does not reciprocate our efforts, it may be time to reevaluate the friendship.

Of course, every relationship goes through ups and downs, and it's important to communicate openly and honestly with our friends. If we notice a change in the dynamic of the friendship, it is worth having a conversation to address any issues or concerns. However, if we find that our friend is unwilling to listen or make an effort to improve the relationship, then it may be a sign that the friendship has run its course.

Letting go of friendships can be difficult, but ultimately,

we must prioritize our own well-being and surround ourselves with positive, supportive people. It's important to remember that as we grow and change, our friendships may also evolve or end. And while it may be a bittersweet realization, letting go of toxic friendships can create space for new, healthier relationships in our lives.

Tips on How to Cut People Out

Cutting someone out of your life can be a difficult and emotionally draining decision. Whether it's a toxic friend, an unhealthy relationship, or a family member who brings nothing but negativity into your life, sometimes removing them from your life is the best option for you. But it's not always easy to do so.

Here are some tips on how to cut people out of your life in a healthy and effective way:

1. Reflect on Your Decision
Before making the decision to end a relationship, it's important to reflect on why you want to do so. Are they consistently causing harm or bringing negative energy into your life? Is the relationship one-sided and draining? It's important to have a clear understanding of why a firm boundary is needed in order for the process to be easier. When life is difficult or we are feeling sad, we often question our previous boundaries because we

experience more self-doubt and lower confidence. Use this book to take notes, and you can reflect back on them later if you question your decisions.

2. Prepare Yourself Emotionally

Cutting someone out of your life can bring up a lot of emotions, so it's important to prepare yourself emotionally beforehand. Allow yourself to feel sad or angry at the loss of the relationship, but also remind yourself that this is ultimately for the best.

3. Communicate Clearly and Firmly

Setting a boundary and ending a friendship can be managed in many ways. You may want to tell the person, or you may want to "ghost" them. Ghosting a person is your decision, but it can be described as slowly distancing yourself from a person without telling them why, such as slowly not replying to text messages in a meaningful way and then not replying at all. Make a decision that is comfortable with you, and how you will feel over time. A lot of people set boundaries in a mean way, and it might not be necessary. After all, the goal of The Friend Cleanse is to gain awareness of yourself and make decisions in relationships that allow you to maintain and grow the energy in your glass. If you choose to hurt someone by "ghosting" them, it may not increase your energy. In some cases, it is the most effective and efficient way to save yourself. Make sure to reflect on your decision before you do it. Boundaries are necessary, but ending relationships has consequences, and can often lead to discomfort or tension. If you choose to speak with the friend you are aiming to disconnect from, be direct and firm in your communication. Let them know that you have made the decision to remove them from your life and explain why. It is important to remain calm and avoid getting into arguments or justifying your decision, beyond your comfort level and energy.

4. Stay Committed to Your Decision
After you set a boundary with someone, it is important to stay committed to your decision. This may mean avoiding contact with them and removing them from social media, or other forms of communication. It can be tempting to reach out or give in to guilt or pressure but remember that this is for your own well-being and long-standing health and energy.

5. Seek Support
Setting boundaries can be a difficult and a very emotional process, especially if you have allowed people to use you or walk on you throughout your life. A lot of empathic people struggle with boundary setting. It is important to seek consistent support from friends, family, or a therapist. Talking about your feelings and having a support system can help you navigate the process and continue your move forward, toward a consistent and healthy relationship sphere.

6. Focus on Your Own Well-Being

Lastly, after setting boundaries with people in your life, it is important to focus on your own well-being. Take care of yourself, engage in self-care activities, and surround yourself with positive influences. Remember that removing toxic relationships from your life can lead to a happier and healthier future, even if it feels icky when the boundary is being set. Make sure to prioritize your own well-being above all else. Cutting people out may be difficult, but it's ultimately an act of self-care and self-preservation. By following these tips, you can successfully remove toxic people from your life and move forward in a positive direction. Remember to be kind to yourself throughout the process and trust that you are making the best decision for yourself. Stay strong, stay committed, and remember that you deserve to live a happy and fulfilling life surrounded by supportive and loving relationships. Keep in mind that setting boundaries is not a sign of weakness, but rather a brave and necessary step towards a better future. Trust yourself, seek support, and prioritize your own well-being to create the life you deserve. Remember, you are in control of who is allowed in your life and it's important to choose wisely. You deserve to be surrounded by people who uplift and support you, and it is okay to let go of those who do not. Stay strong and keep moving forward on your journey towards a happier and healthier life. You are the most important person in your life.

FINAL THOUGHTS

This book is intended to be a helpful exercise that allows us to reflect on the people around us and how they may be adding or draining our glass of energy. My intention is to give you permission to take control of your life and the people within it. We are not the victims of toxic people. We are aware and educated survivors of toxic relationships, and we are able to set boundaries and protect our internal resources. We can model this ability for others, especially our children. We do not need to succumb to peer pressure.

Focus on your own well-being and prioritize it above all else. Take care of yourself. Surround yourself with positive influences. You are strong. You deserve to be happy and in meaningful relationships. Setting boundaries is brave. Trust your intuition. You are in control. Surround yourself with people who uplift and support you, and set boundaries with those that do not.

I once had an epiphany, in a moment when I thought my daughter would be harmed. We were at a park, and we were sitting on a park bench. A man started walking toward us and he was staring at my daughter. I felt uncomfortable and I felt that he was going to harm us. My intuition told me that there was danger in his intention. So, I stood up tall, held my shoulders back, made direct eye contact, and I stepped in front of my daughter. I stood between the man and my daughter. I told the man "Step back," and even I was surprised by the tone of my voice. The epiphany came as a reflection on what I would have done if my daughter was not there on that day, or when I have been threatened on other days. I probably would have stayed seated, looked at the ground, and hoped that I was not going to be harmed. I have done that before in the face of threat. Why was my daughter the permission I needed to stand up, be strong, and protect her and myself? Why was I alone not enough to protect? That was one of many moments in my life, where I decided that I would always protect myself, and in doing so I will protect those people close to my energy and my heart.

ABOUT THE AUTHOR

Dr. Leslie Dobson is a clinical and forensic psychologist in California. She grew up largely in Orange County and then traveled around the world for her education, training, and career. She has worked in some of the most dangerous and difficult settings in the world. Being a young female in forensic psychology, Dr. Leslie focused on her boundaries. She focused a great deal on keeping herself physically safe in these menacing work environments, but also keeping herself emotionally and cognitively shielded when around manipulative people and extremely draining work environments. She focused on her energy, and she learned to check in on her glass of energy every day, in order to assess her strength and the type of boundaries she needed to place around the people in her life. Dr. Leslie continues to work as a forensic and clinical psychologist, and she is a therapist in private practice with a specialty in trauma. She is a mom, wife, and a friend.

Find out more on her website: www.drlesliedobson.com

Made in the USA
Las Vegas, NV
15 February 2024

85825272R00056